The Gospel According to

Mother Goose

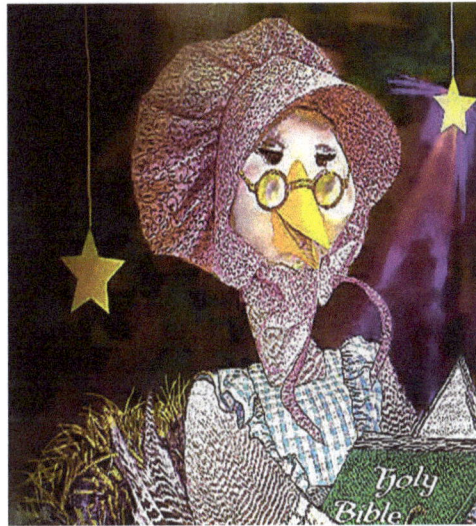

A Journey to Find a Reason for the Rhyme

The Gospel According to Mother Goose:
A Journey to Find a Reason for the Rhyme

ISBN 978-1-940645-76-6

Greenville, South Carolina

PRINTED IN THE UNITED STATES OF AMERICA

Dedication

To my Mom and Dad

Furman and Hallie Hammond
December 2, 1944

It is with much joy that I dedicate *The Gospel According to Mother Goose* to my parents, Furman and Hallie Hammond.

As a child growing up, I remember the happy times Mom and Dad spent with me reading beloved Bible stories and "The Mother Goose Rhymes." These times are special memories for me.

Acknowledgements

**"In all thy ways acknowledge him,
and he shall direct thy paths."
Proverbs 3:6 (KJV)**

A "special thanks" to the following people who made it possible for me to write this book:

- Our Lord and Saviour Jesus Christ, whose sacrifice at Calvary made salvation possible for all who believe.

- My wife, Gail Hammond, who sacrificed our quality time.

- Renee Wright, illustrator, who provided her expertise and talent.

- Judy Hammond, who patiently and graphically designed the book.

- Lois Lucas, who accurately and patiently edited every page of the book.

God bless each of you for your time and efforts to make *The Gospel According to Mother Goose* a reality.

Table of Contents

Foreword

The words on the cover of this book tend to encourage us to continue to read. There may be two things that cause this: the magnetism of the words or the mystery of such a title as *The Gospel According to Mother Goose.* This may suggest that there is something spiritual about the book, even though the original intention of the writers of "Mother Goose" rhymes was quite different. The purpose of this book is to bring together some of the words and characters found in the "Mother Goose" rhymes and those found in the biblical stories. My hope is that each complements the other. Paul Tillich, the great theologian, writes:

> Pictures, poems, and music can become objects of theology, not from the point of view of their aesthetic form, but from the point of view of their power of expressing some aspects of that which concerns us ultimately, in and through their aesthetic form. (1, Int., 13).

As a child, you may or may not have heard the words of the "Mother Goose" rhymes or the stories from the Bible. The values and norms seen in each rhyme have similarities to those found in the stories of the Bible.

There are six areas of ultimate concern which tend to relate to a child's greatest need: security. Those six areas are as follows:

- The Fall
- The Fear
- The Faith
- The Food
- The Following
- The Fate

After a consideration of each part of the title of this book, each of these six areas are discussed. Each rhyme discussed is used to support these areas. More specifically, there is a consideration of the characters, their circumstances, and the consequences. For each story from the Bible used to support these areas, there are some of the same considerations. Paul Tillich says:

> The Bible itself always uses the categories and concepts which describe the structure of experience (1. Int., 21).

One of the source books for the "Mother Goose" rhymes, namely the book entitled *The Original Mother Goose*, does not include page numbering. The supposed number of pages is the page reference. Most of the Scripture references are from the King James Version of the Bible. Any other Bible resources in this book are referenced.

The resources are referenced in the text in one of two ways:

- A pair of numbers (a, b) where "a" is the resource number and "b" is the page number.
- A triple of numbers (x, y, z) where "x" is the resource number, "y" is the volume, and "z" is the page number.

Chapter 1

The Gospel

"The Spirit of the Lord is upon me, because he
hath anointed me to preach the gospel to the poor;
he hath sent me to heal the brokenhearted, to preach
deliverance to the captives, and recovering of sight to the
blind, to set at liberty them that are bruised..."
Luke 4:18

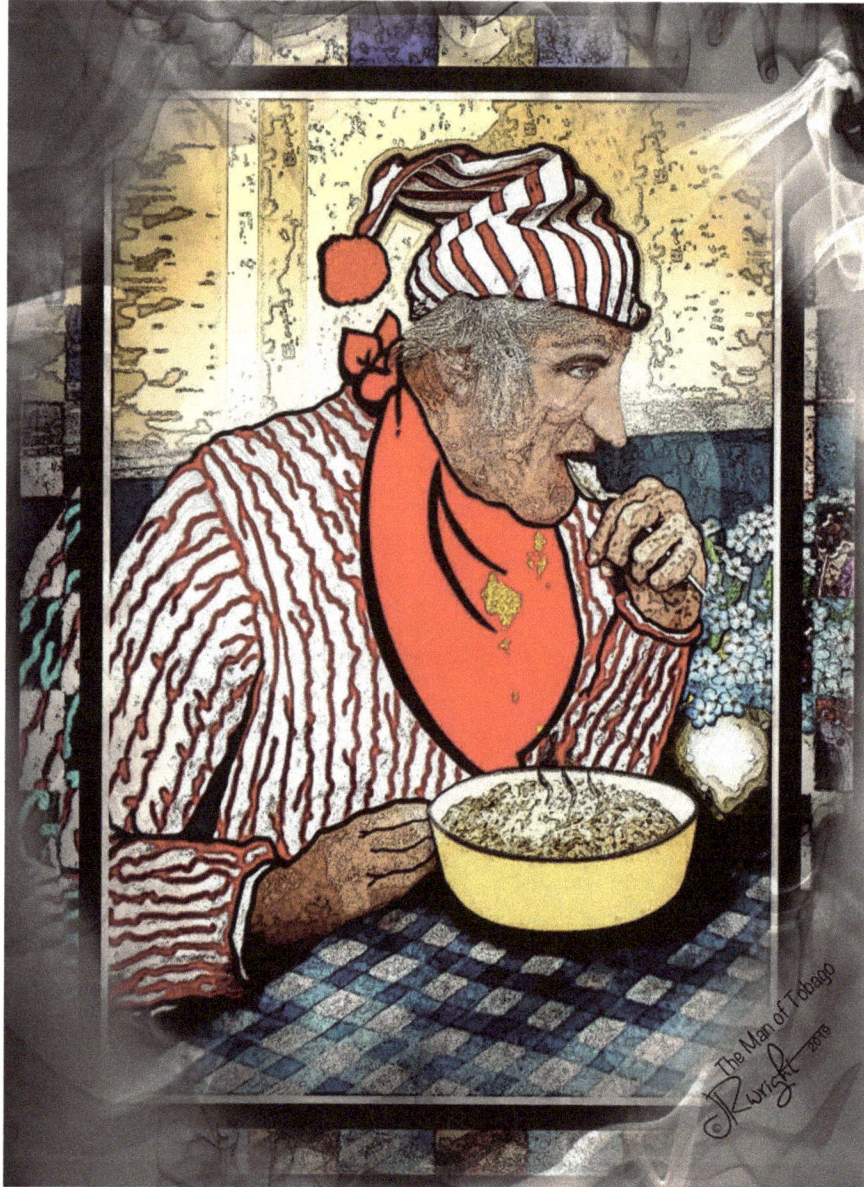

The Man of Tobago

There was an old man of Tobago
Who lived on rice, gruel, and sago;
Till much to his bliss,
His physician said this:
"To a leg, sir, of mutton, you may go." (2, 122)

The Balloon

"What is the news of the day,
Good neighbor, I pray?"
"They say the balloon
Is gone up to the moon!" (2, 111)

The words in the Scriptures are formed to carry with them warm and soothing thoughts meant to raise one's spirits. They can do so only if they are accepted openly. Whether the reader is a parent, a grandparent, or just a close friend, their voice can also communicate that warmth and those soothing thoughts in the reading of Mother Goose. Warmth and soothing feelings mean "good news" to the young listener, since they offer a real sense of security, well-being, and hope. The rhymes of "Mother Goose" and the verses of the Bible, when read, begin to resonate in the minds and hearts of children as they listen. The values felt in the voice of the reader are a vital and valuable part of this process. As the listener becomes secure, they can trust and lean or move toward the words heard as a source of guidance and direction.

Sincere friendships embodying respect and responsibility are key parts of this phase of the journey toward maturity and identity. These friendships also contribute to the process and journey to find a reason for the rhyme and for the words of the Bible. A first impression may be the start of finding a way to approach life and all its mysteries and the hope is that such a method will endure.

With these truths in place, one is enabled to face a difficult and demanding world. The effort to live meaningful and productive lives then results in a healthy physical, mental, and spiritual environment. This comes with a price, that of being very patient. To wait for the maturity in one's body, mind, and spirit can be tough. The prize at the end of such patience is worth the wait. In the framework of one's circumstances, the sound of "good news" leads to a remarkable moment, a defining moment. The moment shapes and molds the remainder of a person's existence on earth as well as his or her essence in the realms of glory.

Shaping and molding are very evident in the Creation narrative in Genesis (the first book of the Old Testament in the Holy Bible). Literal shaping is an implication, but not necessarily the total picture drawn in the text. Creative instincts in the deity do not limit themselves to the first three chapters of the Bible. These instincts contribute to a process that spans all the pages of Scripture from Genesis to Revelation. As the work of "shaping" man takes place, the work of defining the mold in which mankind can be found does too. Some say that people are the products of the environment in which they live. The biblical truth is that people are created through a human process that ultimately redeems itself in and through a Divine process. The process gives mankind hope and reassurance. When the rhymes of "Mother Goose" and the verses of the Bible are considered together, they can actually be very helpful in bringing some "good news" to people who have had only bad news. The person who experiences very difficult circumstances will have a greater appreciation for "good news" than one who has not. There develops over a period of time a sincere longing for any sense of hope that is available to the troubled soul. This results in a greater openness to the idea of the gospel as "good news."

To really understand the word "gospel" as meaning "good news," the readers of this text should first look at some contemporary examples in life that can set the stage for the "good news" that follows. The readers are then encouraged to look at some of the "Mother Goose" rhymes and some of the stories in the Bible. In the world of today, many people already know what "good news" means. For a person who is unemployed, the "good news" is "You are hired." For the person who has had a biopsy, the "good news" is, "It's not cancer." For a person with a tumor, the "good news" is "It's not malignant." For a person who has had cancer, the "good news" is, "It's in remission." For a college applicant, the "good news" is, "You have been accepted." For a doubtful senior in high school, the "good news" is, "You will graduate with your class." For a young woman who has met the one whom she hopes will be the love of her life, the "good news" is the question, "Will you marry me?" For the young man asking the question, the "good news" is her answer, "Yes, I will." For a couple wanting to have a baby, the "good news" is, "You're pregnant!" For the parents who are expecting, the good news is, "It's a boy!" or "It's a girl!" These are just a few of the expressions that one can describe as "good news." They can be found in many places in the "Mother Goose" rhymes and in the stories of the Bible.

The "Mother Goose" Perspective

The "Mother Goose" rhymes have instances which convey the idea of "good news" for those in the rhyme. Today, most people would want to dismiss any connection between the rhymes of "Mother Goose" and the stories of the Bible. The following are two examples from "Mother Goose" which convey a sense of "good news" to the characters in the rhyme.

In "The Man of Tobago," the old man is put on a strict diet. He has been on this diet long enough to be tired of it. He listens as the doctor tells him that he can now eat something more appealing as well as substantial. He can now eat meat. Can you just imagine the effect on those who are sitting at the table with this man? Everyone seated at the table must listen to him concerning his diet. The usual joy that one wants during a meal is nowhere to be found. On the one hand, the family is ready to eat a delicious meal; on the other hand, there is the plight of this man and his diet. To this setting comes the "good news." The diet is no longer needed or necessary; the restrictions have been removed. Those at the table now rejoice with this man and are relieved to hear this "good news."

The man of Tobago is guilty of making some bad choices and has been put on a diet. He is in a state of grief and regret. Even so, he finds relief when he hears the "good news." The burden of guilt is now lifted, and the person is set free. Along with this, the spiritual weight of those past bad choices is lifted. There is a sense of newness to the life that is now to be lived in the context of forgiveness and forgetting.

In the rhyme "The Balloon," the reader will find a question: "What is the news of the day, Good neighbor I pray?" There are two references in this question. The first has to do with the "news of the day." It seems that there must have been some sense of longing to hear the "news" and, moreover, "good news." What follows in the rhyme is the news itself: "They say the balloon is gone up to the moon!" Is there something "good" about this news? Is it simply to produce a sense of wellbeing in the rhyme, or is there something much deeper than that? Looking at the glowing disk in the sky promotes a sense of wanting to "fly to the moon" and be nearer this glowing. The balloon provides a hope which is rooted and grounded in the celestial journey. No one can deny the sight of the moon as a sort of celestial goal. Those who deny the effort to guide a person to the celestial for an eternity cannot deny the aesthetic look at the moon and its neighbors, the stars.

For many hundreds of years, the stars have served to guide those who are navigating their vessels through stormy seas to their destinations. The stars are valuable because of their arrangements, or constellations. Those arrangements have given names. These names bring an almost instant idea of the pattern to expect in the darkness of the night. The study of the stars gives a person the delight of seeing such patterns. The study also provides valuable information to anyone willing to read or to explore. This cognitive journey can be very satisfying and stimulating. It can lead to much in the way of satisfaction and hope.

The Biblical Perspective

The stories of the characters of the Bible are also indicative of "good news" being delivered to people. Several of these stories are shared here:

Noah

In the story of Noah, when the rain comes, the family can now believe the "good news" that their husband and father has been obedient in building the ark. The family gathers together in the ark with many animals. As the rain ceases and the waters recede, Noah and his family accept the "good news" that God has delivered them and that they are safe from the calamity of the drowning waters.

Moses

For Moses, the "good news" is the word of the Lord instructing him to lift his arms. This act of obedience results in a parting of the waters of the Red Sea and the escaping of the children of Israel from the aggressive Egyptians. As the Israelites get to the shore on the other side, the "good news" is that they are safe and secure.

Abraham

For Abraham, who is called by God to sacrifice his own son as a test of faith, the "good news" is that he has passed God's test of his faith and that his son will live. Abraham brings his son, Isaac, to a high mountain to offer this sacrifice. Unknown to his son is the fact that he, Isaac, is to be that sacrifice. Not only does the passing of the test offer "good news" to Abraham; but it also offers "good news" to Isaac.

There are many who are healed and believe. In fact, the first four books of the New Testament are titled "The Gospels" because they share the "good news" stories that Jesus brings to the people of His day. All four books, including Matthew, Mark, Luke, and John, share the stories of the life, person, work, and ministry of Jesus. Countless other people have heard of this "good news" since that time. The words of the Bible, written so long ago, still resonate with the word "gospel," or "good news." Millions of people have heard and responded in a very positive way to the invitation to be the recipient of this "good news," that Jesus is the Saviour of the world. In the Old Testament, the focus is on the salvation of the nation of Israel; in the New Testament, the focus is on individual people who have a personal encounter with Jesus, or His message brought to them through the lives of others.

So, "good news" is an essential part of both our physical and our spiritual psyche. We long for it as we are caught up in the everyday living of life. It is hoped by this writer that the "good news" of Jesus Christ will become an integral part of someone's life experience. That "good news" is that there is help and there is hope now and in the future.

Chapter 2

According to

"Let this mind be in you,
which was also in Christ Jesus..."
Philippians 2:5

Baa, Baa, Black Sheep

Baa, baa, black sheep,
Have you any wool?
Yes, marry, have I,
Three bags full;

One for my master,
One for my dame,
But none for the little boy
Who cries in the lane. (3, 48)

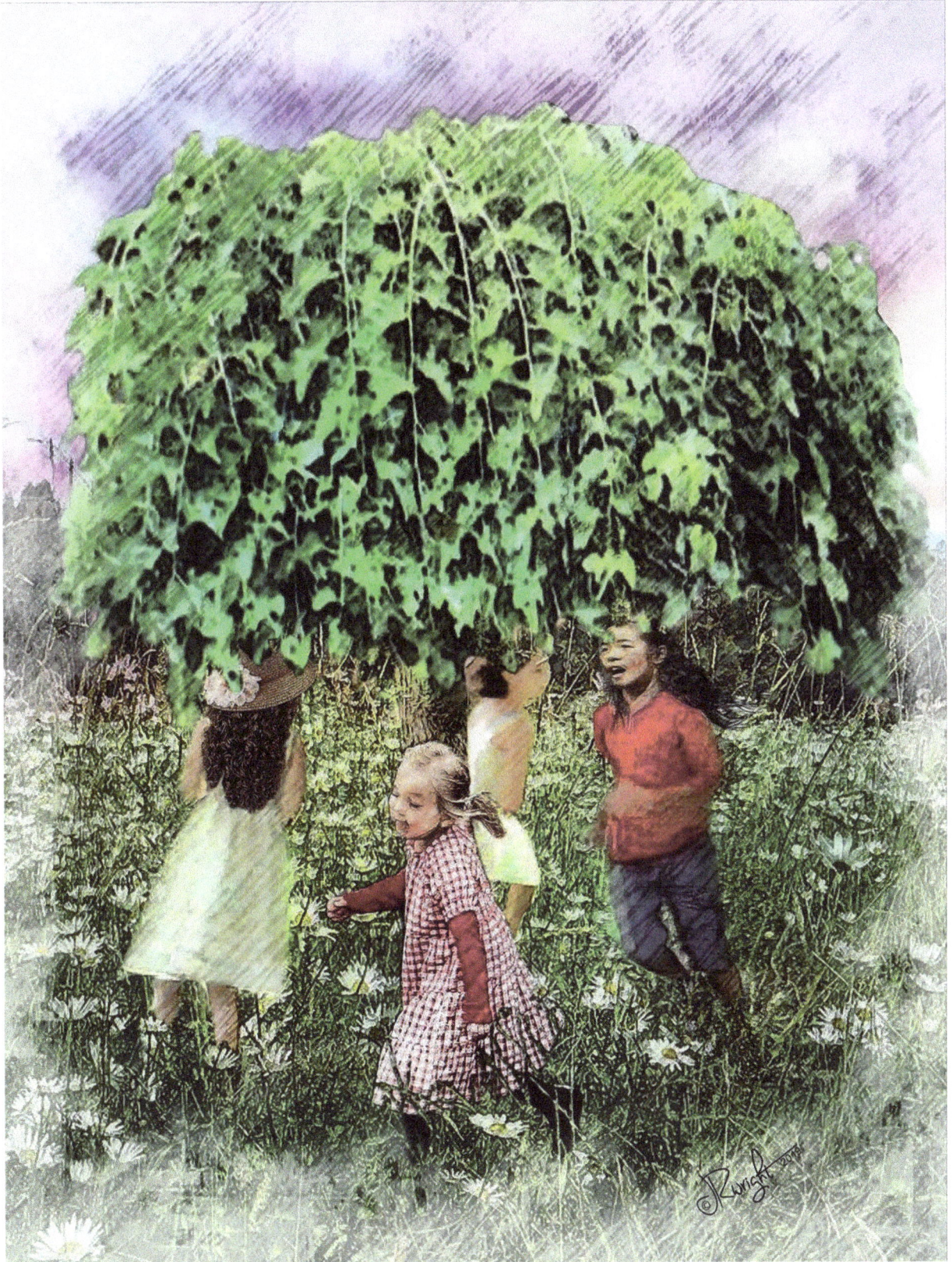

The Mulberry Bush

The Mulberry Bush

Here we go round the mulberry bush,
The mulberry bush, the mulberry bush,
Here we go round the mulberry bush.
On a cold and frosty morning.
This is the way we wash our hands,
Wash our hands, wash our hands,
This is the way we wash our hands,
On a cold and frosty morning.
This is the way we wash our clothes,
Wash our clothes, wash our clothes,
This is the way we wash our clothes,
On a cold and frosty morning.
This is the way we go to school,
Go to school, go to school,
This is the way we go to school,
On a cold and frosty morning.
This is the way we come out of school,
Come out of school, come out of school,
This is the way we come out of school,
On a cold and frosty morning. (3, 55)

In Philippians 2:5, there is a call to harmony or to be in harmony with the mind of Christ. That is the intended goal in using the words "according to" in the names of the first four books of the New Testament:

- The Gospel According to Matthew
- The Gospel According to Mark
- The Gospel According to Luke
- The Gospel According to John

The teachings of Jesus play a vital part in sharing the faith with the world. There is a mandate in the Christian faith to be like Christ. Christians are to incorporate the concepts of respect and responsibility into their relationships with other people. Thinking of the needs of others plays an important part in developing long-lasting relationships as does being conscious of each other's time and space. Even if time and space are momentary realities, the genuineness of one's faith can be measured in part by his or her conscious awareness of others and their needs.

Respect is an attitude. It is defined by the nature of the relationship one has with another. A little child learns to respect the authority of their parent. This is earned by responsible parenting. In the midst of parenting must be reassuring words such as the phrase "I love you." If these words are not found in the actions of the parent, then the child feels alienated and alone. A negative response or attitude can then develop.

Respect is also important in the workplace. A healthy respect is needed for the employees by the management group. A healthy respect is also needed for the management group by the employees.

Work cannot be as effective without such a mutual respect. Companies today are compelled to make sure that this kind of respect on both sides is a reality. Where that is not the case, legal steps are being taken to "encourage" respect as described above.

Responsibility is the action that is the demonstrator of respect. Making sure that there is a right way for all to act is an integral part of responsibility. When one sees that the environment is challenged by a lack of this responsibility, that person is in the position to act. That action is intended to better equip the atmosphere in which they find themselves.

In the home the actions of a parent toward their spouse and their children are an important demonstration of respect. A parent has the responsibility of taking care of their children. Managing their safety and their security is an inherent part of this parental responsibility.

Relationships are formed on the basis of the presence of respect and responsibility. A child does not have to be told that their parents love and respect them. Children have a spiritual "sensor" which alerts them when there is love and respect, and they can "read" that very early in life. When present, love and respect contribute greatly to a child's development. Without that presence, there develops a pathological effect. Something which has the potential to become a normal part of existence now results in a void in one's psyche and leads to an abnormal state.

The harmony that can be found between the rhymes of "Mother Goose" and the stories of the Bible provides great help in finding the "tie that binds" people together. It gives credence to the aforementioned ideas of respect, responsibility, and relationships. The commitment to find this harmony is a part of the intent of this present writing.

The "Mother Goose" Perspective

In the "Mother Goose" rhymes are found the harmony just mentioned. One example is that found in the rhyme "Baa Baa Black Sheep."

One possible explanation for the exclusion of the little boy is his crying. A crying child most often signals that something is wrong. Sometimes, a child uses crying just to get attention because of a critical need. The child may have been left alone. The child may be hungry or thirsty. The child may have been hurt physically. The child may be afraid. The child, if a baby, may need a change. No matter the circumstance, the black sheep had no use for the crying child. The human reality is that not many people like the hearing of a crying child. How does one respond to this sound? Panic. Denial. Escape. Ignore the crying. Frustration. Unfortunately, there is also physical, mental, and psychological abuse. Some people cannot just stand still and let their emotions rule. They are the ones who sense the urgency to help and spring into action to do so. They get the child familiar and supportive company if it is possible. They get the child something to eat or drink. They get the child help for his or her hurt. They assure the child that help is there and there is no longer a danger or threat. They change the diaper. If there is abuse, they get personal help to "get over it" and thereby give the child a chance to live safely and securely.

Human nature wishes the crying to stop. That leads some people to try to solve the problem. Others move away and, in so doing, deny or ignore the problem. The child understands that crying may or may not lead to a reward or to help. In the rhyme, the boy gets no "wool" for crying.

When the weather is cold and frosty, the most susceptible and vulnerable people are children. So, when the rhyme is read, the warmth of the rhyming words removes some of the harshness and dread of cold weather. The warmness tends to soothe the child especially and also connects with the human longing to deal with the cold weather. The cold weather must be dealt with while at home, on the way to school, and on the way home from school.

"Mother Goose" rhymes help to connect the real world to a child in a way that does not alienate the child. A part of that world is any help and hope for which there is a hunger. "Good news" can be a real blessing and a vehicle for the journey to find a reason for the rhyme. In the case of children, it is warmth and security for which they long and it is that which the rhymes bring to the child.

The world of work always includes the impact of weather phenomenon. If people work outside, there is the risk of lightning in a thunderstorm. For this same group, a heavy rain may change the landscape to a muddy mess. Flooding may also be an issue. Strong winds may affect travel, especially flying. Tornados and hurricanes are the greatest wind threats. Making sure that people are kept safe in the work place is a high priority.

For school children, keeping them safe is vitally important. Taking precautions such as fire drills or tornado/hurricane drills can reassure them. Safety at play is vital to protecting children. Doing things on the playground is fine. Keeping the children safe is important as well. Working together as teams and getting exercise are two ways to ensure that children are living healthy lives at school and at home.

The Biblical Perspective

The verses of the Bible can often help the Christian on their journey through life. The first one considered here is found in the Old Testament. It reads as follows:

> The entrance of thy words giveth light; it giveth understanding unto the simple. (Psalm 119:130)

As people proceed on their journey, they search for meaning and purpose. If not, they live in misery. When the words of the Bible verses and the message they convey break through, the people then become more aware of their purpose on earth. An old self is then transformed to a new self and to a new life. This process is the intent of the verse that led off this chapter and the verse just presented. Gradually, a person becomes that which they are created to be. The insight of the theologian Paul Tillich can again be very helpful:

> Universals can become matters of ultimate concern only through their power of representing concrete experiences. The more concrete a thing is, the more the possible concern about it. The completely concrete being, the individual person, is the object of the most radical concern — the concern of love. (2, II, 211)

People respond to various forms of love. They move away from what they see as a false sense of love, and they move toward a genuine sense of love. When the connection is made, there can be a powerful response on the part of most human beings. There are exceptions, but the vast majority of humankind does respond to love. Love can and does conquer all.

The Bible maintains a connection between reality and the understanding of it. In Proverbs 16:22, the writer says, "Understanding is a wellspring of life unto him that hath it..." It does help the quality of life experienced by humankind. The context of faith in daily experiences gives life a much deeper and richer meaning. In 1 Samuel 14:7b, the writer says, "Do all that is in thine heart: turn thee; behold, I am with thee according to thy heart."

The best example of a journey is in the Old Testament story of the Israelites. Moses has been called to lead them out of Egypt to their destination: The Promised Land. On this journey, there is a real sense of connectedness at times and, at other times, a real sense of disconnectedness. As Moses connects with God, he sometimes disconnects himself from the people. As he connects with the people, he then disconnects himself from God. This is seen in the story of securing water for the people. They are quite thirsty and let Moses know that they are thirsty. They neither see nor hear Moses while they are thirsty. Then Moses becomes impatient with God and strikes the rock to quicken the stream of water. Then the water flows freely.

In the New Testament, Paul writes to the Corinthian church, suggesting that the membership "be perfectly joined together in the same mind and in the same judgment" (1 Corinthians 1:10b). Spiritual oneness is sometimes a naïve attempt to avoid painful confrontation. Here, Paul projects a future that is sound when people work together in Christian love. "We are human!" some will say, and they are right. This makes the process take on a greater imperative: to resolve the issue. It is our humanness that alienates us; it is our divinity that leads us to resolution. Luke, the doctor, quotes Jesus when He says, "...thou hast hid these things from the wise and prudent, and hast revealed them unto babes..."

(Luke 10:21b). The Bible describes people who have been Christians for a short time as "babes." These are people who have had little experience in the faith and are hungry to apply the truths in Scripture to their lives. Through the years, this yearning for connectedness grows and it is a part of the process of spiritual maturing. One evidence of this yearning is found in the words of Paul also written to the Corinthian church:

> Eye hath not seen, nor ear heard, neither have entered into the heart of man, the things which God hath prepared for them that love him. (1 Corinthians 2:9)

So, the Scriptures do not attempt to alienate us from reality, nor its experiences. Their purpose is to heighten the awareness of the reader concerning the elements of reality in them. These elements include all sickness, pain, stress, loneliness, depravity and any other physically, mentally, or emotionally-charged components of reality. What can and should happen is an improved awareness of life that allows for a discovery of its meaning as one continues their journey. This meaning should become deeper every day that the Christian lives.

Chapter 3

Mother Goose

"She looketh well to the ways of her household,
and eateth not the bread of idleness.
Her children arise up, and call her blessed..."
Proverbs 31:27-28a

Since the late 18th century, "Mother Goose" has been a literary phenomenon. There was a publication referred to as *Mother Goose's Tales* in 1729. The first known book of Nursery Rhymes was published in 1744. It was not until 1780, however, that a publication associated the name "Mother Goose" with rhymes. The use of "Mother Goose" became a serious incentive for publishers, printers, and people in general to attach the reference to an "old woman," known by some as an "old witch." Publishers and writers tried to assert their ownership of "Mother Goose"; none had any outright proof of ownership. A detailed look at the chronological history of the evolution of the name "Mother Goose" is presented and supported in this book.

A Partial History of "Mother Goose"

French literature had in its history several references to "Mother Goose." Jean Loret (1610-1665) used the term "Mother Goose" to refer to a collection of stories appearing in a monthly periodical in 1650, *La Muse Historique*. The reference line was *"Comme un conte de la Mere Oye,"* which translates to the line "Like a Mother Goose story." In 1697, a book containing several folk tales was published by Charles Perrault, a Frenchman. Those tales included "Sleeping Beauty," "Little Red Riding Hood," and "Cinderella." On the title page of the book were the words *"Contes de ma la mere l' Oye,"* which were translated as "Tales of Mother Goose." There were no rhymes of "Mother Goose" as they are known today in the book.

The English literary body of publications about "Mother Goose" contained much more in references and in rhymes. In 1729, Perrault's tales were translated by the Englishman Robert Samber and published that year. The new title was *Mother Goose's Tales.*

In 1744, the first known collection of "Mother Goose" rhymes was published by Mary Cooper in London and was called *Tommy Thumb's Song Book*. Later that year, John Newbery, a book seller and publisher, published *The Little Pretty Pocket Book*. He dedicated the book to all "the Parents, Guardians and Nurses in Great Britain and Ireland." As success entered the picture, Newbery realized that this publication could lead to others, ushering in a profitable endeavor. So, he continued publishing these works and, in 1766, introduced his most famous publication, *Little Goody Two Shoes*. In 1780, Thomas Carnan, the stepson of John Newbery, became owner of Newbery Publishing House. Sometime after Newbery's death in 1767, Thomas Carnan entered a work at the London Stationer's Hall. The book entitled *Mother Goose's Melody; or Sonnets for the Cradle* contained fifty-two rhymes, each accompanied by a black and white drawing to illustrate the content of the rhyme. These were traditional English nonsense songs and rhymes. In addition, Carnan included sixteen verses from Shakespeare which enhanced the market value of the publication.

A few years later, pirating brought the Newbery Mother Goose to America. In 1786, Isaiah Thomas was the first American editor to publish with proper authority a book of "Mother Goose" rhymes, namely, "Mother Goose's Melody." In 1878, *Mother Goose in White* was published. A year later, *The Old Fashioned Mother Goose Melodies* was published. In 1916, these were re-published by Rand McNally & Company and the publication given the title *The Real Mother Goose*. In 1928, *Mother Goose Nursery Rhymes,* with the arrangement by Logan Marshall, was published in Chicago, and the rhymes contained therein were illustrated by Julia Greene. As late as 1958, *The Space Child's Mother Goose*, written by Fredrick Winsor, was published in New York. The contents were illustrated by Marian Parry.

The Biblical Perspective

In the stories of the Bible, there are many references to mothers and to their role in shaping and molding their children's faith in God. There are passages that genuinely exemplify the calling of God for women with children to be godly mothers. One such passage is found in the book of Proverbs, chapter 31. Solomon tells of the virtues and values of the woman who answers God's call to so live:

"Who can find a virtuous woman? for her price is far above rubies. The heart of her husband doth safely trust in her, so that he shall have no need of spoil. She will do him good and not evil all the days of her life. She seeketh wool, and flax, and worketh willingly with her hands. She is like the merchants' ships; she bringeth her food from afar. She riseth also while it is yet night, and giveth meat to her household, and a portion to her maidens. She considereth a field, and buyeth it: with the fruit of her hands, she planteth a vineyard. She girded her loins with strength, and strengtheneth her arms. She perceiveth that her merchandise is good: her candle goeth not out by night. She layeth her hands to the spindle, and her hands hold the distaff. She stretcheth out her hand to the poor; yea, she reacheth forth her hands to the needy. She is not afraid of the snow for her household: for all her household are clothed with scarlet. She maketh herself coverings of tapestry; her clothing is silk and purple. Her husband is known in the gates, when he sitteth among the elders of the land. She maketh fine linen, and selleth it; and delivereth girdles unto the merchant. Strength and honor are her clothing; and she shall rejoice in time to come. She openeth her mouth with wisdom; and in her tongue is the law of kindness. She looketh well to the ways of her household, and eateth not the bread of idleness. Her children arise up, and call her blessed; her husband also, praiseth her. Many daughters have done virtuously, but thou excellest them all. (Proverbs 31:10-29)

The woman in this profile of a godly mother (and wife) does all that she can to keep a God-centered home for her whole family. Everyone in the family receives a great amount of respect. This respect is evident in the effort that she makes daily. For His inspiring of godly mothers, to God be the glory!!

The list of books about "Mother Goose" is extensive. The value of these rhymes, spoken of earlier in this text, remains high in the minds and hearts of children and adults. Children can identify with the children in the rhymes, and adults can remember those rhymes read to them. For all who read or listen, it is an unforgettable experience.

Notes

Chapter 4
The Fall

"And many among them shall stumble,
and fall, and be broken..."
Isaiah 8:15a

Humpty Dumpty

Humpty Dumpty

Humpty Dumpty sat on a wall,
Humpty Dumpty had a great fall;
All the King's horses, and all the King's men
Cannot put Humpty Dumpty together again. (2, 30)

Jack and Jill

Jack and Jill

Jack and Jill went up a hill,
To fetch a pail of water;
Jack fell down, and broke his crown,
And Jill came tumbling after. (2, 121)

Early in life, people become concerned about falling. This concern is sometimes brought on by an actual fall, or the sight of someone else falling, or the thought of falling. When there is a fall, there is the great possibility of some form of injury: skinning a hand, skinning an arm, or hitting a head. All of these imply pain, distress, and a feeling of isolation. To see someone else fall causes us to feel what is felt by them. Maybe the sight of the fall creates sensitivity for their pain and their isolation. Maybe the seer can sense their needs. This is cause for them to want to be helpful. These emotions are evident in both the "Mother Goose" rhymes and the Bible stories. There is also the "fall" which happens when a person becomes attracted to another person. Often the feeling is mutual, and the dating and mating process begins. On other occasions, the feeling is not mutual. This process can be an agonizing time in the life of the "fallen." Support by friends, family, and others encourages the complete repair of the brokenness. This process involves time and it certainly does involve patience. Church families and fellow Christians can play a vital role in the putting-back-together process. There can be help and there can be hope.

The "Mother Goose" Perspective

One of the "Mother Goose" rhymes which focuses on falling is "Humpty Dumpty." Humpty Dumpty is sitting on a wall and suddenly he has a great "fall." From a sense of superiority and togetherness, he descends to a sense of inferiority and brokenness. From the pedestal of being "up and in," he falls to the low estate of being "down and out." The writer confirms this when there is an indication that even the most powerful of royalty could not restore Humpty Dumpty to his lofty height.

In the days when kings ruled their kingdoms, a major responsibility of the kings was to protect their subjects. Upon the fall of Humpty Dumpty, even the king's best efforts do not help or heal the brokenness experienced by Humpty Dumpty. There is here a sense of urgency, and there is a sense of desperation. The destiny of the fallen one becomes an even greater issue as time passes. Helplessness breeds hopelessness. Fortunately, not every "broken" soul is helpless. There are steps to lift the spirit of the person who has been hurt. Determining the source, detaching one's self from the source, and doing things that strengthen are the steps which help to heal the hurt or brokenness.

The other "Mother Goose" rhyme chosen to focus on falling is "Jack and Jill." When a person reads this rhyme, they picture a hill where there is a well. Along comes a boy named Jack and a girl named Jill. They are given the "chore" of getting a pail of water. What they are to do with the water is not clear. What is apparent is that they are very close friends. Some illustrations even picture them walking up the hill hand in hand.

After Jack has filled the bucket with water, he goes back down the hill. He may not have calculated the shift in weight brought on by a filled bucket of water. The increased weight on one side throws him off and he falls. The rhyme also speaks of the consequence when it reads, "He broke his crown." The implication is a brain concussion. Whatever the case, Jack is hurt because of the fall. Jill also falls and may be hurt. The rhyme does not say; however, there is the thought that she is hurt. Falling and pain can be linked together and certainly are in this rhyme. Many times, patients in hospitals are referred to as being a "fall risk." That means that if they are left unattended, they may fall. If they fall, they may break a bone or have a concussion (as mentioned above with Jack). In either case, excruciating pain can result. Valuable time must be spent evaluating and pursuing the right regiment of medicine and treatment which is truly an inconvenience to all involved.

The Biblical Perspective

The Good Samaritan Helps the Fallen

In the story of the Good Samaritan a fellow human being falls. Some translators say that he "fell among thieves." He is indeed experiencing great pain. After the priest and the Levite ignore him, a man comes along to help. Jesus describes him as a "certain Samaritan." This passerby, having seen the need and feeling the sense of his own obligation, moves toward the wounded man and offers his help. As he does, this Jewish man begins to drop his effort to alienate and begins to cooperate. The Jewish people and the Samaritan people have built a cultural wall that separates them from each other. As the injured traveler is helped, he begins to lower his sense of alienation and attempts to reconnect with the one who is willing to offer help and hope.

The Good Samaritan binds up his wounds, places him on his donkey, and takes him to an inn for the night. He also pays for the injured man's lodging and promises the innkeeper that he will repay any additional expenses on his next visit. These actions bring hope to the injured man. When a person is severely beaten, there is a loss of trust in humanity. The hope of renewed trust now becomes a reality.

Jesus Confronts Simon Peter

There can be a spiritual fall in the life of a person. This happens at the Last Supper when Jesus confronts Simon Peter. Jesus shares with him the thought or the idea that he, Simon Peter, will deny Him three times before the rooster crows. Simon Peter takes offense at such a suggestion. Later, he will indeed "fall" from the pinnacle of his spiritual loftiness. Even as Jesus is led to His crucifixion, Simon Peter denies that he knows Him three times. He also denies being a follower of Jesus, that is, one who is associated with Him as a disciple. On the third occasion of these denials, the rooster crows, and Simon Peter remembers the words of Jesus and is repentant for what he has done. Simon Peter recovers from his spiritual "fall," perhaps on his own or through his fellowship with other believers.

The characteristic that seems to accompany a "fall" is regret. The decision to act in a certain way or to posture one's self in a certain way sets up a person for a "fall." After the fall, there is regret. The decision is not a good one. The posture is not a good one. The person then seeks help for the hurt. In the story of Simon Peter, there is indeed regret and he is remorseful. He regrets that he has denied knowing Jesus. He begins the steps of a spiritual recovery that lead him to be a true disciple of Jesus. His work for the Kingdom of God helps others who are themselves in a "fallen" state.

Children often fall and cannot rescue themselves from this fallen condition. They immediately seek help in the only way they know. They cry out! As adults people often cry out too. The church is just one of the agencies that can come to their rescue. Those people who call themselves Christians can be there and help by nurturing and caring for the fallen. Hope then is clothed in help. As a person helps another, there is a sense of belonging to humanity again. The person who has "fallen" now reconnects with others, taking away the sense of alienation and loneliness that they feel. As a person reconnects, they begin to focus on a new sense of belonging. This belonging leads to a sense of peace that lives within them. This peace complements their feeling of hope.

Notes

Chapter 5

The Fear

"Fear not, little flock; for it is your
Father's good pleasure to
give you the kingdom."
Luke 12:32

Little Miss Muffet

Little Miss Muffet

Little Miss Muffet
Sat on a tuffet,
Eating of curds and whey;
There came a big spider,
And sat down beside her,
And frightened Miss Muffet away. (2, 29)

The Mouse and the Clock

The Mouse and the Clock

Hickory, dickory, dock!
The mouse ran up the clock;
The clock struck one,
And down he run,
Hickory, dickory, dock! (2, 115)

Fear is a real issue for little children. Some of their fears are overcome, while others are processed with the help of those who care. A child cannot function when they are afraid, and neither can an adult. Fear causes discomfort, uncertainty, and insecurity. It robs people of their confidence and their identity. Fear often changes the way in which someone views life. People become suspicious of others when they are afraid. They become defensive in their attitudes and in their actions. These fearful ones no longer use their best senses to assess situations in which they find themselves. Hasty decisions are made without any regard for others or for their well-being. Some people, when trapped or paralyzed by fear, cannot move in any direction. They simply must remain still until help arrives.

In the warmth of a rhyme, there is help in finding comfort, certainty, and security. Finding comfort, certainty, and security will better enable the child to grow and mature. Even if fear is not removed, the presence of others with the right attitude assists greatly in the process of growing and developing the child's skills that lead to maturity. Fear does impact us and, the earlier that fact is realized, the better for all concerned.

The "Mother Goose" Perspective

In the "Mother Goose" rhymes are many references to fearful circumstances. The reading of these rhymes can change the attitude of the listener. To sense the presence of the reader and the sound of their voice is one way for the child to overcome the effects of fear on their lives. One of the "Mother Goose" rhymes that relates a "fearful" situation is "Little Miss Muffet."

Little Miss Muffet sat on her "tuffet." This is more than an effort to rhyme; it is an effort to identify the location of where she sat. The general idea is that she is sitting and eating her lunch. She is very unaware that a spider is nearby. As she eats the meal, the spider comes down and "sits" beside her. Who knows whether a spider can sit or not? The very presence of the spider created the circumstance that evoked fear in the mind of this little girl. She immediately leaves for a safer and more secure location. After hearing this rhyme, the listening child is encouraged to have a plan when the circumstances warrant. To run away is one plan; to be attentive to those involved in one's surroundings is another way. Either way, the listener gains some confidence and security in the knowledge of a plan concerning what to do. Knowing those involved and their behavior cannot hurt.

Another "Mother Goose" rhyme which reflects the circumstances surrounding fear is "The Mouse and the Clock." Mice can be found in many places around the house. Whether in the attic, in the basement, under the house, or in any number of places in the rooms of the house, mice are there. In cabinets, couches, and yes, even in clocks, mice are often seen or heard.

In this rhyme, the mouse has run up the clock and is doing well. The mouse feels secure in this place of adventure and hiding. Then the clock strikes one. The proximity of the mouse to the sound amplifies the effect and the mouse "runs" back down the clock. The place of security and safety has turned into a place of insecurity and danger (at least in the mind of the mouse). Fear takes control of the behavior of the mouse. The mouse regains peace of mind and a safe and secure environment. Fear then can be seen and identified for the listener. The listener feels the effect of being startled by a sudden loud noise. A child relates well to this unannounced interruption to their life. The small mind, even with limited life experiences, still senses the effect of that moment. His or her own experiences come to mind as listening to the rhyme occurs. The closeness to the one who is reading helps to secure the highly impressionable listener. The warmth of the rhyme soothes both the body and the soul of the listener.

The Biblical Perspective

Fear in the narrative of the Bible takes on two basic forms: the meaning is uneasiness and tugging of the nervous system or the meaning is a healthy respect and reverence for the subject, that subject usually being the Lord God.

Jesus Calms the Storm

The disciples are accompanying Jesus across the Sea of Galilee. Jesus has gone below in the ship to take a nap. He is very tired from the efforts that He has made to minister to the needs of the people around Him. While He sleeps, a storm at sea comes up and all the passengers and crew grow very anxious for their safety. They become fearful for their lives. Some of them find Jesus asleep and awaken Him. They question His sleeping while the storm is raging. Jesus calmly speaks and the storm ceases. The fellow passengers then feel a sigh of relief.

The Fear of the Centurion

As Jesus faces His crucifixion, a centurion sees Him. The writer Matthew says, "Now when the centurion, and they that were with him, watching Jesus, saw the earthquake, and those things that were done, they feared greatly, saying, 'Truly this was the Son of God.'" (Matthew 27:54)

The thought of deity brings an attitude of respect, referred to by the writers of Scripture as "fear." This respect is clothed in the former meaning of fear, that of having one's nerves shaken by the events occurring at the time. The writer of Proverbs says, "The fear of the

Lord is the beginning of knowledge..." (Proverbs 1:7). Whether the context is insecurity or respect, fear is real in the mind of the fearful. Fear remains real to all!

Chapter 6

The Faith

"Now faith is the substance of things hoped for,
the evidence of things not seen."
Hebrews 11:1

I See the Moon

I See the Moon

I see the moon,
And the moon sees me;
God bless the moon,
And God bless Me. (3, 74)

Christmas Is Coming

Christmas Is Coming

Christmas is coming, the geese are getting fat,
Please to put a penny in an old man's hat;
If you haven't got a penny a ha'penny will do,
If you haven't got a ha'penny, God bless you. (2, 123)

In the spiritual realm, a person neither sees nor hears. They can hope only in the spiritual realm. The reference here is being able to rise above the circumstance and see out of the valley in which they find themselves. The reference is also being able to hear something that soothes one's soul. Those goals come about only in the context of faith. Looking beyond and seeing the "way" comes only through relationships that develop and last for many years.

To be able to call on others in the time of need is another step in the process of having faith. A lack of certainty is to be replaced as a starting point. Many people today have faith because someone cared about them. To awaken out of the sleep of worldliness is another move toward the realm of faith. To see the faith of others brings strength and courage to the effort a person is making to get over any one of life's hurdles. In all these situations, a sense of despair because of earthly circumstances is turned into a sense of hope. The need to leave worldliness behind or to see the faith of others in action means that *faith is real.*

The "Mother Goose" Perspective

The "Mother Goose" rhymes shed light on the phenomenon of faith. The first of these rhymes is "I See the Moon." A child looks at the moon and sees the light of the moon. The moon is not a light; it is an opportunity for the sun to shine upon it. The result is a bright spot in the darkness of the night. The moon does not have eyes, yet it "sees" the child. Mutual respect between child and moon happens in the world of the child. Added to this is the blessing that only God gives. The faith of a child is real. The moon may not have shined on this child for very long, yet this child accepts the joy of seeing that light. On one occasion Jesus said, "Whosoever shall not receive the kingdom of God as a little child, he shall not enter therein" (Mark 10:15b). When a child hopes, the light of a silvery moon reaches into their mind and heart to usher in that hope.

Children are fascinated by the lights in the sky whether it be the sun, the moon, or the stars. They point to them in awe of what they see, and they reach out as much as possible with their little arms. There is something mystical and magical in the skies above, and they want to be nearer to the cosmos than the body allows. This begins their journey of faith in all aspects of life, including that of the things in the sky. While they sense the limitations they have, they still seek for the help and hope that comes by "moon watching." During the most critical times in their lives, the faith perspective in the psyche begins to "shine" forth, and it gives them help and hope.

In the rhyme, "Christmas Is Coming," an old man is begging. An appeal is made to the listener and/or the reader to give money to help this man. The condition is that the giver can give what he can afford to give. If the person reading/listening cannot afford to give money, the writer of the rhyme invokes a blessing from God upon him or her.

Any child who has experienced Christmas does not have to be given an explanation. By faith, he or she must wait since they do not see this holiday, and they do not yet hear the music of the Christmas bells. Given their child-like faith, the Christmas experience ignites the joy and happiness that Christmas brings. Parents assist in the offering of this hope by promoting the idea of Santa Claus. They have hope, a hope brought about by those past experiences around the tree. This experience lays the groundwork for a faith perspective. The child begins to experience the nature of faith as divinely created. Christmas has that inherent faith perspective. This is the day and the season set aside to celebrate the birth of Jesus, the ultimate symbol of one's faith in God.

The Biblical Perspective

There are many stories about women of faith in the Bible. The stories show that women of faith strongly believe in the power of God. This power is most supremely expressed in the life and teachings of Jesus Christ. Two stories of special women illustrate that the work of Jesus is seen in the lives of others. These women seek His healing power in the life of someone very close to them or in their own lives. Their faith perspective is quite evident in the way they approach and address Jesus.

The Canaanite Woman

In the first case, that of a Canaanite woman, the help of Jesus is sought for her daughter. The concerned mother describes the daughter as being "cruelly tormented by a demon." In today's world, it can mean a mental breakdown, the effect of great anxiety, or a deep depression. Whatever the case, the mother's appeal brings with it a certain sense of desperation. Jesus does not respond to her immediately; however, she is desperate enough to challenge the disciples to do something. She does not lose respect for Jesus, for she continues to refer to Him as "Lord" and as "the Son of David." She does not want anything to obstruct her effort to make an appeal to Jesus to heal the body of her daughter. They then ask Jesus to "send her on her way." Jesus makes known to her that His present ministry is focused on the people of Israel. That fact does not stop her. She pleads by saying, "Help me!" Sometimes, pride gets in the way of people asking for help. For this woman, pride neither stops her nor discourages her.

Jesus recognizes her faith by saying to her, "O woman, great is thy faith..." (Matthew 15:28). From that point on, healing comes to the daughter. Is this healing simply physical, or is it mental, or is it spiritual? The Bible does not say so directly, but indirectly, it is the faith of this Canaanite woman that brings healing to her daughter.

The Personal Appeal of a Woman

A second story of the faith of a woman focuses on the spiritual impact of putting one's faith in Jesus. A Pharisee invites Jesus to have a meal at his home. Jesus goes to the home, enters, and reclines at the table. In those days, they did not "sit" at the table; instead they reclined on something like a sofa. Two people recline in such a way that they are close enough to carry on a meaningful conversation. A woman of the town, a very sinful woman, comes to the house, enters, and moves close to Jesus. She brings with her an alabaster jar of fragrant oil and stands behind Jesus at His feet. She washes His feet with her tears and wipes them with the hair on her head. She then kisses His feet and anoints them with the oil. The Pharisee, in a jealous and judgmental tone, points out that this woman is a sinner and is not to be touching Jesus.

Jesus then tells the story of a man who has two debtors. One of them owes him a lot of money and the other man only a small amount. Neither of them can pay the man back, so he forgives both their debts. Which of the debtors owes him more? The answer is the man who borrows more. Jesus acknowledges the correctness of those who hear Him and respond. He then reminds the host that nothing is done for Him when He enters the house: no water, no kiss of greeting, and no fragrant oil. The woman has many sins and is forgiven. That's why, indeed, Jesus indicates that she loves Him more than the others nearby. He says to her, "...Thy sins are forgiven" (Luke 7:48b). Later He said, "...Thy faith hath saved thee; go in peace" (Luke 7:50b).

These stories illustrate in a biblical way the impact of faith on the lives of people. People are dramatically changed physically, mentally, and spiritually. Faith gives us help and hope as we live in the circumstances of our lives.

Notes

Chapter 7

The Food

"...when I was hungry, you gave me food;
when thirsty, you gave me drink..."
Matthew 25:35 (NEB)

Jack Spratt

Jack Spratt
Could eat no fat,
His wife could eat no lean;
And so,
Betwixt them both,
They licked the platter clean. (2, 37)

Little Jack Horner

Little Jack Horner
Sat in the corner,
Eating of Christmas pie:
He put in his thumb,
And pulled out a plum,
And said, "What a good boy am I!" (2, 80)

Food is a great concern of all human life, all animal life, and all plant life. To be able to live, a being must have food and water. The ability to obtain food is a part of the training to live. To be able to hunt for food or to cultivate food through farming or gardening is an absolute necessity. This absoluteness makes obtaining food an ultimate concern. The food we eat today has been "glamorized" by television and other media. Food now has become a hot market item in stores and restaurants everywhere. The goodness of food today rests in the "comfort" received by the customer. Food is tried in the court of public opinion and scrutiny. This trial serves our culture well, for that act of being seen and experienced by the public causes the food industry to "step up" and do the best they can to impress. That which is fashionable seems to delight more than that which is healthy. People have that need to be "entertained" while they eat. For those less fortunate, the ideas above are foreign and insulting to their circumstances in life. They simply are hungry and need nourishment to survive. For the less fortunate, food is an immediate concern as well as an ultimate concern.

The "Mother Goose" Perspective

In the "Mother Goose" rhymes, food is also a real concern. Many references are made to the need for food. Two rhymes have been chosen to illustrate the point. The first of these is "Jack Spratt." In this rhyme a couple can eat all the meat. Both are restricted in their diet choices. Jack probably is suffering from problems stemming from poor circulation. The fat accelerates the buildup of plaque in his arteries. His wife is possibly suffering from some heart disease which involves too much iron in her food. This causes her to have to watch her food intake. If this caution is left unheeded, there is a possibility of an earlier death. For the wife, eating lean meat involves a health risk. To leave something on one's plate has always been accompanied by warnings or challenges to "clean" one's plate. Taking out more than a person needs to eat is thought of in some circles as a "sinful act"; it certainly borders on being a social taboo. To be greedy in taking too much food is frowned upon by those charged with guiding the little ones. To eat a healthy diet is a noble goal for all humanity.

People do not gather around the table today like they did many years ago. Diverse schedules and the desire for independence and self-sufficiency contribute to this practice. There are those who still gather to eat and discuss the events that concern them from day to day. Sometimes, there is so much involvement in the discussions that someone later says, "Did we eat?" The important thing is that people do find much to help them as they sit around the table. The world's problems are not solved, but the people involved face the world with hope.

The second rhyme is "Little Jack Horner." What is going on with this little boy? There is a lot of speculation about the picture drawn by this rhyme of "Mother Goose." The writer of this text suggests two possibilities: First, here is a little boy who makes it a part of his mischievous psyche to stick his thumb in the pie, which has been made by his mother for Christmas dinner. She is busy and wants to complete the preparations for the meal. So, she puts the pie in a place reserved for pies. Jack knows where the pie is and goes for it. He gets caught! The punishment is to sit in the corner and eat that whole pie (maybe!). Jack is a survivor. His well-intentioned mother is not going to get the best of him. He must replace the dread of the punishment with some reassuring words, so he pulls out a plum and says, "What a good boy am I?" Second, there is a more positive possibility: Jack has completed all the cleanup chores for the family to come for Christmas. (His mother is busy with the food.) She rewards Jack with one of those highly desired plum pies. He goes to the corner and begins to eat. In his gloating thoughts about being "good" he says, "What a good boy am I?" Hunger for the pie drives Jack to pursue a taste of it, and he risks it all just for some of that pie. Sometimes, great risks and pains must be taken to get food. In the first depiction of the rhyme, Jack risks the closeness to his mother. In the second depiction, the risk involves an alienation from friends who hear through their own mothers about Jack's "good" behavior.

The Biblical Perspective

Many people believe that the food they eat is a blessing from God. As a symbolic gesture of their thanks, people stop and share their gratitude with a prayer which is "the blessing." Even children say something like the following:

> God is great,
> God is good.
> Let us thank Him for our food.
> By His hands, we all are fed.
> Give us, Lord, our daily bread.
> Amen

The Israelites

In the Old Testament after God promises to provide food, Moses says of the "manna," or bread, that he and the other Israelites see: "This is the bread which the Lord hath given you to eat" (Exodus 16:15b). Food is necessary for physical and spiritual growth. The physical food God provided during the Exodus brings nourishment and sustenance to the people of Israel. The spiritual food brings encouragement to the Israelites in their belief that God does provide. During the time of the exodus of the Israelites, the loneliness and despair causes these people in great transition to question their faith. Any sign of God's working in their behalf is a welcome part of their pilgrimage to the Promise Land. To give up is physically and spiritually fatal. To hold their heads up and move forward in faith results in the success of finding a new homeland for the Israelites. When Moses gives the glory to God for the food He provides, that act lifts the spirits of those nomadic people.

Jesus Breaks the Bread

Jesus meets His disciples in an upper room for the last supper. The supper comes just one day before His crucifixion. In Matthew 26:26, the writer says that He "took bread, and blessed it, and brake it, and gave it to the disciples..." He then says to His disciples, "This is my body." The symbol has a spiritual tone. It calls upon the disciples to believe Him concerning the punishment that He is about to face. They are called to trust Him and believe in the cause for which He later suffers. His suffering *is* the debt for the sins of all humanity. Jesus soon suffers and dies, and it brings spiritual chaos to the disciples. They are men of faith, trained by Jesus, and prepared by Him for these moments. Spiritually speaking, the disciples and other followers of Jesus find real nourishment in the fact that Jesus is willing to die for them.

Both physical and spiritual food provide a real source for keeping a life healthy and happy. Properly balanced diets contribute to mankind's health; properly balanced spiritual diets (Bible reading and prayer) contribute to mankind's happiness. So, food is a very important part of a child's world and an adult world. For a child, the desire for food comes before a desire to learn about the world in which they live. It comes before a child's ability to say, "I'm hungry!" It comes before a child knows about the love of those close to them. Hunger is one of the earliest urges that children have.

In the "Mother Goose" rhymes and in the stories of the Bible, there are many references to hunger. In this chapter there are several rhymes and stories that have been discussed. Satisfying hunger with food comes early in life. As a person grows, the desire for spiritual food develops, given the right amount of instruction and encouragement. This is not about indoctrination. This is about the spiritual nourishment for which mankind has long sought. In the biblical stories, people seek physical and spiritual nourishment. In today's world, people still search for and find nourishment for the body and for the soul.

Notes

Chapter 8

The Following

"And he saith unto them, 'Follow me, and
I will make you fishers of men.'"
Matthew 4:19

Mary Had a Little Lamb

Mary Had a Little Lamb

Mary had a little lamb,
Its fleece was white as snow;
And everywhere that Mary went,
The lamb was sure to go.

It followed her to school one day,
That was against the rule;
It made the children laugh and play
To see a lamb at school.

And so the teacher turned it out,
But still it lingered near;
And waited patiently about
Till Mary did appear.

"Why does the lamb love Mary so?"
The eager children cry.
"Why, Mary loves the lamb, you know,"
The teacher did reply. (3, 103)

The Crooked Sixpence

The Crooked Sixpence

There was a crooked man
And he went a crooked mile;
He found a crooked sixpence
Beside a crooked stile;
He bought a crooked cat
Which caught a crooked mouse,
And they all lived together
In a little crooked house. (3, 33)

Human nature reveals the fact that there are leaders and there are followers. A leader must have a "split" vision. One eye is to keep track of the path on which the leader journeys, and the other eye is to keep track of those people who are following. If a leader only thinks of where they are going, there may be none that follow. If a leader only keeps track of those who are following, then the leader's path may be a "crooked" one. Some of these thoughts are reflected in the "Mother Goose" rhymes and the biblical stories which follow. Consider the path of one who pays strict attention to that path. There is no sense of adjustment to the needs of those nearby. There is also no sense of adjustment to what one experiences along their spiritual path.

Suppose the leader nurtures the needs of those who are following. Those needs are always under the microscope of the leader. If the least bit of circumstances jeopardizes the journey of the follower, the leader takes immediate action to rectify the situation. In either case, adjustments must be made to balance the role of the leader.

The "Mother Goose" Perspective

There are two "Mother Goose" rhymes which depict the idea of a leader or follower relationship. The first one is "Mary Had a Little Lamb." This rhyme has a lot of symbolic significance in connection with the idea of leader and follower. What causes a leader to be so effective? It is the ability of the leader to relate to the followers. The fourth verse basically sums up this idea. Why does a person or thing follow another? The answer is in the respect and responsibility each has for the other.

Mary does not prevent the sheep from following her. In fact, the verse implies that the "cleanliness" of the sheep is enough to make the following genuine. The complete devotion of the sheep adds to the quality of the sheep's commitment to follow. Typically, sheep are not allowed at school, yet Mary patiently accepts the idea of the sheep being there even though the rule forbids it. The children at school very quickly accept the idea of the playful sheep. The happiness is heard in their laughter and their acceptance is seen in their play; they do neither when they are threatened.

The teacher pictures the impact of the acceptance of this sheep. She or he sees many children bringing their "pets" to school, and the results are chaotic. So, the teacher puts the sheep out of the school. The sheep does not go far. In fact, the sheep waits patiently for Mary to appear. Followers are often encouraged to be patient. Leadership sometimes requires thought and training. The disciples of Jesus are to become leaders of the movement to offer salvation to a lost world, and they need training. Jesus uses a hillside as a "classroom" to teach them using the "Sermon on the Mount" (Matthew 5-7) as His lesson plan.

Some people believe that the world is crooked. Children do not have the cognitive nor the experiential skills to make such a statement. They do know in some sense when something is crooked. As they grow, they become more aware of the crookedness of the world. The association of things seen as crooked and people seen as crooked becomes more real as time passes.

In the rhyme "The Crooked Sixpence," a crooked man "followed" a crooked path. He may have gone more or less than a mile since the measure is suggested to be "crooked." On this path he found a sixpence, which is "the sum of six (old) pennies" (4, 1342). The sixpence is beside a crooked stile. A stile is "a step or set of steps used in climbing over a fence or wall" (4, 1407). What does this verbal picture suggest so far? This man does everything wrong. The sixpence is a payoff that allows someone to cross over a fence. The wall is designed to prevent entry. The wall is constructed in a crooked way by intent or by lack of skill. The intent may have been to challenge the owner's privacy. Otherwise, the step or steps are built crooked because of an absence of a skilled carpenter or mason. The man does not stop there; he buys a cat which has a malady of some sort. However, the cat can overcome the malady enough to catch a mouse. In all this crookedness, these creatures manage to live.

The world may be crooked, and the inhabitants may be crooked too. The mandate for humanity is to find a sense of harmony and togetherness. That search can be carefully and correctly orchestrated with the proper sense of leadership and follow-ship. Humanity still hungers and thirsts for help and hope.

The Biblical Perspective

Isaiah

Two stories in the Bible have a direct connection with the idea of following. The first involves the story of Isaiah as a prophet to the people. Isaiah refers to those religious people of his day as "ye that follow after righteousness" (Isaiah 51:1). The assumption is that the prophets have the first five books of the Old Testament (often referred to as the Pentateuch) to read and study. This meditative privilege gives Isaiah the foundation he needs to be able to speak in both a challenging and encouraging way. The people are apt to listen and to "follow" the words of the prophet Isaiah. With the background of those first five books of the Old Testament in place in their minds and hearts, they mature more quickly or take part in a more intense following.

The Disciples of Jesus

In the second story, Jesus is calling His disciples. More particularly, the calling of the two brothers, Andrew and Simon Peter, to "follow" Him begins His invitation to serve. This is the challenge given to them in the lead-off Scripture for this chapter. Jesus uses language familiar to these men. They know what it means to fish. There is sacrifice and sweat equity in the fishing business; and Jesus knows that in ministry, there is also sacrifice and sweat equity. Jesus knows what it takes to reach them and encourage them to "follow" Him.

What ideology a person follows is a great concern from day to day. Parents are concerned about the peer pressure faced by their children and the persons whom they will "follow" if they are not leaders. This concern continues well into their adult years.

Chapter 9

The Fate

"For God so loved the world,
that he gave his only begotten Son,
that whosoever believeth in him should not
perish, but have everlasting life."
John 3:16

Little Bo-Peep

Little Bo-Peep

Little Bo-Peep has lost her sheep,
And can't tell where to find them;
Leave them alone, and they'll come home,
And bring their tails behind them.
Little Bo-Peep fell fast asleep,
And dreamt she heard them bleating;
But when she awoke, she found it a joke,
For still they all were fleeting.
Then up she took her little crook,
Determined for to find them;
She found them indeed, but it made her heart bleed,
For they'd left all their tails behind 'em!
It happened one day, as Bo-Peep did stray
Unto a meadow hard by —
There she espied their tails, side by side,
All hung on a tree to dry.
She heaved a sigh, and wiped her eye,
And over the hillocks she raced;
And tried what she could, as a shepherdess should,
That each tail should be properly placed. (2, 1)

Cock Crow

Cock Crow

Cocks crow in the morn
To tell us to rise,
And he who lies late
Will never be wise;
For early to bed
And early to rise,
Is the way to be healthy
And wealthy and wise. (2, 68)

In John 3:16 is found the best description ever written of the fate of the believer. Certainly, to most people, there is a concern for their own fate or destiny, as they continue their journey on earth. John clearly states the words of Jesus as he, John, addresses the issues of eternal security. This "fate" is another indicator of what a person might describe as an "ultimate concern" in life. Along with the other five (fall, fear, faith, food, and following), there is a growing attention paid to this matter of fate. To visualize a person's fate is impossible; to prepare a person's soul for eternity certainly is possible. Embracing God's plan of salvation brings peace of mind to the "believer" and provides help in "seeing" beyond this life. People cannot draw a complete picture without faith. Taking a "faith step" allows the believer to find their place in the picture that will ultimately be painted. This is the purest and truest form of faith. This faith is in the concept that a person has of who the deity is. The image is not the essence. The essence is in the reality of a spiritually superlative being. Mother Goose rhymes give the reader some insight into the process of journeying to the great beyond. Bible stories also paint some faith pictures to guide people on their celestial journey.

The "Mother Goose" Perspective

"Mother Goose" rhymes often depict the fate of someone or something. The rhymes give a picture of the consequence of a person's actions and the punishment they suffer. For example, the crying boy receives no wool due to his crying period. Jack Spratt takes on a non-fat diet because he recklessly eats as he pleases. Humpty Dumpty falls because he tries to be above all others or to be better than others.

In the "Mother Goose" rhyme "Little Bo-Peep," the main character, Bo-Peep, has lost her sheep. She does not know where they are. She becomes tired and falls asleep. She dreams that she hears them. On awakening, they are still lost. She becomes more determined to find the lost sheep and goes her way to do so. She strays from the herd and finds the tails hanging on a tree to dry. She takes the tails and tries in vain to return each tail to its proper place.

Lostness is not new, for many have been lost since the beginning of time. Restoring one to the herd becomes the main priority in the life of the shepherd. Sometimes, he or she thinks of the process of finding the lost sheep as more important than finding food or water. That idea must be carefully weighed on the scales of simplicity to be considered as a fact. Whatever the case, Bo-Peep knows that she must find the sheep and she will give the task all of her being, or all that she has.

The parallel of "lostness" in the world of sheep and the world of humanity is quite apparent. Humans must become acquainted with the impact of lostness to be a part of the process of "saving" the universe. The recovery of lost individuals leads to the recovery of that structure called the "heavens and the earth." Mankind can ill afford to ignore this basic thought.

In the "Mother Goose" rhyme "Cock Crow" is an endorsement for getting enough sleep at night. There is no need to be concerned about oversleeping. The crowing of the rooster is the signal to get up and begin a new day. The words that follow the getting up are an appeal for the person listening. He or she understands that there is no wisdom reserved for those who sleep late. Wisdom has always contributed to happy and productive lives. Even children want to be wise about life. Early in their development, children begin to seek approval, acceptance, and affirmation. These things come to those who "learn" life as early as possible. By doing so, they are wise for having learned this life lesson.

In the second verse of this rhyme, there is a plan for becoming "healthy, wealthy, and wise." The two-step process involves going to bed early in the evening and getting up early in the morning. This leads to the development of a spirit that is strong, a body that is healthy, and a mind that is sound. Together, these attributes produce a well-tuned life which is to be lived productively and successfully. What better fate is there than this? There is none.

The Biblical Perspective

In the Gospel of Luke (chapter 15:1-32), there are three stories that address the issue of "lostness." These stories deal with the impact of losing something or someone (including one's self). These stories are among a group of stories that Jesus tells His disciples and followers. These stories are called "Parables." The purpose of Jesus telling these stories is to address a certain spiritual reality with an everyday story. The listener may not have related to the concept without the familiarity of the story. The ultimate purpose is to impress upon these listeners the importance and the urgency of the subject. In this case, the fate of the followers of Jesus becomes His ultimate concern. His desire is that they have hope as He later leaves them.

The three stories (Parables) are as follows:

- The Parable of the Lost Sheep
- The Parable of the Lost Coin
- The Parable of the Lost Son

A brief look at each of the stories will confirm the intention of Jesus to get the message to His disciples and followers. His hope is that they connect the teaching of the Parables about "lostness" and the value of finding faith in God.

The Lost Sheep

A shepherd discovers that one of his many sheep has strayed from the flock. This is an interesting indicator of how concerned shepherds are about their sheep. Upon the discovery that one has "strayed," the shepherd leaves the flock and searches for the lost sheep. When he finds the sheep, the sheep will often crouch down to defend against the impending punishment. The shepherd reaches down and takes two feet in each hand, places the sheep on his shoulders, and carries it back to the flock. The hope is that the sheep will become reacquainted with the other sheep and "follow" the shepherd where he leads them.

The Lost Coin

A young woman has lost a coin. In the story the woman may have been engaged to be married. Rather than giving a ring, ten coins are a sign to a woman of her engagement. If one of the coins is lost, then she can no longer claim to be engaged. When she discovers that a coin is "lost," she begins to look all over her house for the coin. The finding of the coin means that she now can share her joy of the discovery and her hope for a happy life that awaits her marriage.

The Lost Son

This parable relates the story of a family that has two sons. The younger son grows tired of the family routine and desires a life of his own. He goes to his father and asks for the portion of the inheritance that is his. The custom is that the older son gets an additional part of the estate. Since there are two sons, the elder gets two parts and the younger son gets one part. The father reluctantly gives the younger son his part. The younger son takes his part and moves a great distance away. He lives it up and eventually spends all his money. He becomes hungry and must work just to survive. He finds a job feeding swine or hogs. One day, he comes to himself and decides to go back home. His thought is that the servants at his father's house live better than he. When he arrives home, his father welcomes him with open arms. The father even throws his son a party because he thinks his son has died and yet he is alive.

The fate of humanity has been an ultimate concern throughout the time of man's existence. Not knowing what the future holds has a way of getting the attention of men and women that have lived upon the earth. Both the "Mother Goose" rhymes and the stories of the Bible address the "lostness" of people and things, and they leave the reader and the listener with a sense of hope that someone cares enough to seek the one who is lost. Alienation caused by lostness is replaced by association brought on by togetherness.

Epilogue

"Let that therefore abide in you,
which ye have heard from the beginning.
If that which ye have heard from
the beginning shall remain in you, ye
also shall continue in the Son, and in the Father."
1 John 2:24

The subject matter presented in this book has been given the title *The Gospel According to Mother Goose*. The subtitle is *A Journey to Find a Reason for the Rhyme*. From the "Mother Goose" rhymes and from the stories in the Bible, the question arises, "What can we conclude about the subject as presented?" There is no intent to connect the "Mother Goose" rhymes with the stories in the Bible. Even so, the cultural imbedding of certain ultimate concerns cannot and should not be denied. Mankind today still seeks answers to the questions raised by his or her own existence and experience. Some people ignore the questions. Other people conveniently design their own answers to life's ultimate questions. This designing becomes their "journey" to discover the meaning of life. Is there then a reason for the rhyme? For the person on the Christian "journey," there certainly is a reason and that reason is a desire for security whether temporal or eternal. This desire leads to the warmth and soothing sound that comes from a reader whom the child trusts. This is a temporal expression of a temporal reality. The eternal reality comes with the process of relating to the words and deeds of those whom we know, trust, and love. If that person cannot be trusted, then neither can their faith perspective.

Many younger adults today cannot see the faith (especially the Christian faith) because they do not see that faith in the lives of those closest to them. We cannot blame these younger adults! We simply must act toward them in a way that causes them to develop a hunger and a thirst for what makes us who we are. As they see us act, these younger adults begin to desire the quality of life seen in us; and the sight of us occurs when we genuinely "walk the walk" and not just "talk the talk."

What are the things that a person can do to bring about this hunger and thirst for faith? In Micah 6:8 the prophet Micah suggests three things, and they are for the person who is on a journey to find a reason for living a meaningful life here on earth. First, the person is to "do justly." The fair treatment of others around us makes a big difference. Making sure that there is impartiality in dealing with others is quite important. Giving others the benefit of the doubt helps them to see that there is the possibility of just treatment. The values and norms we are taught by Jesus help us to assess others. We are to follow His leadership by practicing the truths expressed in what we have read in the biblical stories. Second, the person is to "love mercy." It is one thing to be merciful to those around us out of a sense of duty; it is quite another to forgive others because Jesus forgives us. Showing mercy in times or circumstances deserving punishment speaks volumes to those who see our lives from day to day. Third, the person is to "walk humbly with their God." This "walk" is another reference to the life earlier described as a "journey." Our walk or journey through life is to be done in a way that expresses the humility described by Micah. The very presence of the thought or spirit of God is enough to make life a humbling experience.

In the New Testament, Paul the Apostle and missionary visits many places and churches. (These churches are in the homes of fellow Christians where people gather together and worship.) One church is Thessalonica, and Paul writes to this body of believers encouraging them with these words:

"... I pray God your whole spirit and soul
and body be preserved blameless unto
the coming of our Lord Jesus Christ."
1 Thessalonians 5:23b

Paul describes in this verse the real concern that all humans have about their spirit, soul, and body. A major part is played by the mind, which is the control center of a person's thoughts and the actions that follow. The heart of a person is really the control center of their emotions. Any faith development that occurs on a person's journey is through the heart.

These discussions and considerations lead us to firmly believe that there is a reason for the rhyme. That reason is for the God in whom we believe to reach out to us and walk with us throughout our lives no matter what circumstances may occur in our lives. That journey begins with the warmth of a nursery rhyme in the lives of some who hear the "Mother Goose" rhymes read. As a person grows physically, mentally, and emotionally, a "leap of faith" occurs. At that point, our lives become more attentive to the spiritual answers for life's ultimate concerns.

An Invitation to

Become a Disciple

If you have a desire to become a Christian or follower of Jesus Christ, these are the steps that will lead you into your journey:

- Realize that you are a sinner, a person who has disobeyed the laws of God.
- Repent of your past life, or express regret and remorse for your past actions and attitudes.
- Respond by willingly committing your life to Jesus Christ.
- Relate to others as seen in the life of Jesus.

(Print your name in the first blank and your signature in the second blank.)

I, _____, agree to take these steps to find meaning in the life of Jesus, to enrich my own life, and to experience salvation through Jesus Christ now my Saviour and Lord.

_____ on _____
          (Signed)   (Date)

Resources

Acknowledgements
1. The Holy Bible (KJV), Nashville, TN: Holman Bible Publishers, 2010.

Foreword
1. Tillich, Paul, *Systematic Theology*, Three Volumes in One, New York: The University of Chicago Press, Harper & Row, Publishers, 1967.

Chapter 1
1. The Holy Bible (KJV), Nashville, TN: Holman Bible Publishers, 2010.
    - Luke 4:18

    The Scripture references for the stories used in the Biblical Perspective are listed below:
    - Noah: Genesis 8:1-14
    - Moses: Exodus 14:21
    - Abraham: Genesis 22:1-12

2. Wright, Blanche Fisher, Illustrator, *The Original Mother Goose*, Philadelphia, PA: Running Press, 1992.

Chapter 2
1. The Holy Bible (KJV), Nashville, TN: Holman Bible Publishers, 2010.
    - 1 Samuel 14:7b
    - Psalm 119:130
    - Proverbs 16:22a
    - Luke 10:21b

- 1 Corinthians 1:10b
- 1 Corinthians 2:9
- Philippians 2:5

2. Tillich, Paul, *Systematic Theology*, Three Volumes in One, New York: The University of Chicago Press, Harper & Row, Publishers, 1967.

3. Wright, Blanche Fisher, Illustrator, *The Original Mother Goose*, Philadelphia, PA: Running Press, 1992.

Chapter 3

1. www.rhymes.org.uk/mother-goose-origins.htm

2. The Holy Bible (KJV), Nashville, TN: Holman Bible Publishers, 2010.
    - Proverbs 31:10-29

Chapter 4

1. The Holy Bible (KJV), Nashville, TN: Holman Bible Publishers, 2010.
    - Isaiah 8:15a

    The Scripture references for the stories used in the Biblical Perspective are listed below:
    - The Good Samaritan: Luke 10:30-36
    - Jesus Confronts Simon Peter: Matthew 26:31-35

2. Wright, Blanche Fisher, Illustrator, *The Original Mother Goose*, Philadelphia, PA: Running Press, 1992.

Chapter 5
1. The Holy Bible (KJV), Nashville, TN: Holman Bible Publishers, 2010.
    - Proverbs 1:7
    - Luke 2:10b-11
    - Luke 12:32

    The Scripture references for the stories used in the Biblical Perspective are listed below:
    - Jesus Calms the Storm: Mark 4:35-41
    - The Fear of the Centurion Soldier: Matthew 27:54

2. Wright, Blanche Fisher, Illustrator, *The Original Mother Goose,* Philadelphia, PA: Running Press, 1992.

Chapter 6
1. The Holy Bible (KJV), Nashville, TN: Holman Bible Publishers, 2010.
    - Mark 10:15b
    - Luke 7:48b, 50b
    - Hebrews 11:1

    The Scripture references for the stories used in the Biblical Perspective are listed below:
    - The Canaanite Woman: Matthew 15:22-28
    - The Personal Appeal of a Woman: Luke 7:36-50

2. Wright, Blanche Fisher, Illustrator, *The Original Mother Goose,* Philadelphia, PA: Running Press, 1992.

3. Fujikawa, Gyo, *Mother Goose,* New York: Sterling Children's Books, 2007.

Chapter 7

1. The Holy Bible (KJV), Nashville, TN: Holman Bible Publishers, 2010.

    The Scripture references for the stories used in the Biblical Perspective are listed below:
    - The Israelites: Exodus 16:15
    - Jesus Breaks the Bread: Matthew 26:26

2. Wright, Blanche Fisher, Illustrator, *The Original Mother Goose*, Philadelphia, PA: Running Press, 1992.

3. New English Bible, The Oxford University Press, The Cambridge University Press, 1961.
    - Matthew 25:35

Chapter 8

1. The Holy Bible (KJV), Nashville, TN: Holman Bible Publishers, 2010.
    - Matthew 4:19

    The Scripture references for the stories used in the Biblical Perspective are listed below:
    - Isaiah: Isaiah 51:1
    - The Disciples of Jesus: Mark 1:16-20

2. Wright, Blanche Fisher, Illustrator, *The Original Mother Goose*, Philadelphia, PA: Running Press, 1992.

3. Fujikawa, Gyo, *Mother Goose*, New York: Sterling Children's Books, 2007.

4.	Agnes, Michael, Editor in Chief, *Webster's New World College Dictionary*, Fourth Edition, Cleveland, OH: Wiley Publishing, Inc., 2006.

Chapter 9
1.	The Holy Bible (KJV), Nashville, TN: Holman Bible Publishers, 2010.
    - John 3:16

    The Scripture references for the stories used in the Biblical Perspective are listed below:
    - The Lost Sheep: Luke 15:4-6
    - The Lost Coin: Luke 15:8-9
    - The Lost Son: Luke 15:11-24

2.	Wright, Blanche Fisher, Illustrator, *The Original Mother Goose*, Philadelphia, PA: Running Press, 1992.

Epilogue
1.	The Holy Bible (KJV), Nashville, TN: Holman Bible Publishers, 2010.
    - 1 John 2:24
    - Micah 6:8
    - 1 Thessalonians 5:23b

About the Author

Michael Eugene Hammond ("Mike") was born in Monroe, North Carolina, to Furman Samuel and Hallie Smith Hammond on April 27, 1946. Mike had no brothers or sisters. The family moved several times in Union County, North Carolina, Lancaster County, South Carolina, and Green Cove Springs, Florida, before settling in Lancaster County in the summer of 1954. At the age of ten, Mike accepted Jesus Christ as his Lord and Saviour at Ebenezer Baptist Church, Lancaster, South Carolina. On Mother's Day, 1960, the family moved their letters to Taylor's Grove Baptist Church.

Mike graduated from Lancaster High School in Lancaster, South Carolina. After finishing high school, Mike earned the Associate in Arts Degree from Wingate College (now Wingate University), the

Bachelor of Science Degree from Wake Forest University, the Master of Divinity Degree from Southeastern Baptist Theological Seminary, and the Master of Arts Degree in Mathematics at Winthrop University, Rock Hill, South Carolina.

Mike has served the Lord in various places and in various capacities. While in school, Mike was youth director of two churches: Boulevard Baptist Church, Raleigh, North Carolina, and First Baptist Church, Lancaster, South Carolina. In the spring of 1970, Mike was called to be pastor of Zoar Baptist Church near Warrenton, Virginia. The Zoar church family sent a request to Mike's home church, Taylor's Grove Baptist Church, asking them to ordain him into the Gospel Ministry. Mike's ordination took place in the spring of 1970. In the fall of 1970, the ministry to Zoar Baptist Church ended because of the distance from Southeastern Seminary. In the spring of 1971, Mike was called to be pastor of Republican Baptist Church, a position he held until December 1972.

From 1973 until 1977, Mike was pastor of Providence Baptist Church in the Kershaw Association. From 1977 until 1981, Mike taught at Winthrop University in the Mathematics Department. In 1979, he was the supply pastor of Faith Baptist Church in Clover, South Carolina. From 1981 until 1989, Mike taught at various colleges and universities on a part-time basis. For one year (1982-83), he was a full-time faculty member at Winthrop University, Rock Hill, South Carolina, and for one year (1986-87), he was a full-time faculty member at Queens University in Charlotte, North Carolina. For several months in 1984 and in 1988, Mike was the interim pastor of Bethel Baptist Church, Lancaster, South Carolina.

Mike first spoke at Beaver Creek in July 1966. Rev. Steve Neal asked him to supply for him while he was on vacation. In November 1989, Mike went to Beaver Creek Baptist Church to supply for two

Sundays. On the first Sunday in September 1990, Mike was called as pastor of the church. During his ministry at Beaver Creek, Mike met and married Gail Bowers Hammond on May 30, 1992. At the end of May 2002, Mike resigned as pastor from Beaver Creek Baptist Church. For three years during his pastorate, he also held a full-time position on the faculty of Frances Marion University in Florence, South Carolina. Also, during his ministry at Beaver Creek, Rev. Hammond was the preacher for the Annual Session of the Moriah Baptist Association. His text was 1 Corinthians 13:8-11.

In the fall of 2002, Mike was called to University Baptist Church as their pastor. That role lasted for thirteen months. Then the family joined Heath Springs Baptist Church and attended there until June 2004. It was then that Mike became pastor of Jones Crossroads Baptist Church, Lancaster, South Carolina. On September 17, 2017, Mike retired from Jones Crossroads.

Mike served as a part-time instructor in Mathematics at Wingate University in Wingate, North Carolina, from 2002 until 2019. From 2004 until 2007 and from 2010 until 2011, Mike served as a math instructor at Grace Academy, Matthews, North Carolina.

Mike and his wife, Gail, now reside in Heath Springs, South Carolina.

Through the years Mike has served in the Moriah Baptist Association in various capacities including the following: President, Pastors Conference; Vice Moderator; Moderator; Associational VBS Director; Chairman, Moriah Golf Tournament Committee; Budget Committee; Personnel Committee; Nominating Committee; and the Committee on Committees. Mike is currently serving as Moriah's Historian and as a member of the Personnel Team.